Original African American Names:

Undefined

Original African American Names:
Undefined

By Adrienne N. Bryant

Original African American Names: Defined by Adrienne N. Bryant

Book Cover: Cynthia Martin Designs

Published by Adrienne N. Bryant, Denver, CO.
To contact author visit : www.originalafrican americannames.com
Email: oaan2014@gmail.com

ISBN:13: 978-1494305505
ISBN-10: 149430550X

Original African American Names: Undefined

Original African American Names: Undefined

Dedication

I dedicate this book to the millions of young people who on behalf of their love ones carry their original African American names proudly.

You are my inspiration.

Forward

My mission to encourage young people to add a definition to their original African American names began with one party list and one lesson plan many years ago. The party list was a list of invitees to my child's birthday party. The list of names came from my son's kindergarten teacher. I carried that list with me for over thirty years. That list of names sparked my interest in unusual names. At the time, it was just a fascination that I could not let go. How could I know that this would all come together in a book to honor children with original African American names?

Years later, in my second career as a teacher, I had planned a literacy lesson with an activity on the naming process. In retrospect, I realize this was a critical and pivotal point in my journey to writing *Original African American Names: Undefined.* I had asked my sixth grade students to research their name meaning and write about their names. The lesson required my students to look up the meaning of their names. I provided a stack of name books, in good faith, only to discover the limitations of the selection. In 1997, many of the books did not even recognize the names of half the students in my class. That year, I reassured my students with original African American names, that I would write a book with their names and their meanings. Thus, my mission was born, with no clear pathway to accomplish my promise.

This book, *Original African American Names: Undefined* has in it the original names that I have encountered over the years. It is hardly a representation of every original name. Nor does it represent every original name I have come across over the last 30 years. My process has been imperfect and sporadic. Basically, the process was whenever I came across a list of names, I would peruse it for that interesting sounding unique name. Yearbooks and sports rosters were wonderful sources. Then, there were those occasional names that I would hear on a television program, or read in a magazine. Sometimes, I would get an opportunity to speak to the namer or namee, learning first hand that the name was indeed created. In every encounter, the person I spoke to was excited and pleased to know that their original name would someday day be documented in a book.

As I became solely interested in original names, I developed a way to verify names using websites and books that offered name meanings. If the name was authentic (belonging to a real person) and did not have a meaning, it was a candidate for *Original African American Names: Undefined.* Just as my students had searched for their names in name books during that challenging lesson in 1997, I would search for their name again in several name books.

This process gave me a unique insight into the name book industry. I discovered several books with original names, while many more name books omitted original names entirely. Several name books went one step further to discourage original African American names.

Omission of original names, in my judgment, perpetrated the American quasi-caste system adding names to skin color and social economic status as a means of oppressing. No child chooses their skin color, economic status or name. Yet in a very perverse way, some Americans have found a way to add names to deny access. Articles, comedy routines and YouTube videos verify these vicious attacks on individuals with original African American names.

I began to realize that by the time students with original African American names were in middle school, many were defensive, defenseless or resolute about their unique names. These were young people who for six years or more endured the mispronunciations and judgments about their original African American names. At the same time they innately knew that somehow their names were extraordinary. They knew their names were given in love and a desire for them to achieve. Bearers of original African American names are truly ready and excited for a change in the dialogue; a positive acknowledgement of their unique names.

Original African American Names: Undefined honors the creativity of parents or naming surrogates who for whatever reason decided not to choose a "used" name. A name burdened with the baggage of the previous owners. Parents or naming surrogates, themselves, likely were raised without the benefit of centuries of ancestral culture and language. Yet, these parents or naming surrogates tapped into a brilliant, unabashed and unshackled creativity to choose a name unlike any other name. Original African American names fly or falter with their own name history.

In my judgment, the first step was to create a name; the next step is to assign a meaning; and finally, I would like those creative names to come alive with their naming story. There are so many of you with original African American names who may have never considered your power to define yourself with your unique name. It is so important to let you know, that your story is unique and powerful. Let this book pave the way to the next steps.

I challenge each person I encounter who has an original name to define their name and document their story. Reclaiming an ancestral practice of naming with a definition and a ceremony is an act of empowerment. This empowerment is validated with documenting. Documenting the naming stories is essential to understanding the historical paradigm shift from adopting names of others or names created by others to embracing your own originality or the originality of the individual that named you. I would like to build a resource and a network to empower individuals with original African American names to define their names, to share their naming stories, and culminate those two acts into a naming ceremony.

> 1. Define your name.
> 2. Share your story
> 3. Participate in a naming ceremony.

Original African American Names: Undefined is a reference book for those interested in cultural competence in dealing with individuals with these unique names. All can encourage individuals with undefined names to add a meaning. My desire is that everyone with an original African American name would take this opportunity to add a meaning to their name. In the back of this book you will find a positive word list that I believe will be useful in selecting an appropriate meaning. You can contact me by email, Face book or Twitter to be featured in my next book.

Original African American Names: Undefined, fulfills part of my promise to put original African American names in print. But I now need Avondre, Chaniya, Trevon, Kniamiayah, Marquan, Nacreasha, and all the others with original African American names listed in this book to come forward. I need you to document your positive and empowering meanings in the next book. That book will be dynamic and inclusive of many original names not just the names I collected. Together we will create a powerful and positive acknowledgement of individuals with original African American names.

I would like to acknowledge Reshae and Davihon. They were the first to document their name meanings on a cell phone video recording in 2010. Reshae means 'power'. Davihon means 'strong in athletics'. I love what these two young people have done. The names 'Reshae' and 'Davihon' will be in the next book along with their chosen meanings and with everyone else who chooses to place a meaning and story with their original name and submit it prior to the publication deadlines.

Finally, I want to acknowledge all of the individuals who decided to create a name. It is your Kuumba (Creativity) that *Original African American Names: Undefined* honors. Your names make our culture more beautiful. Your names demonstrate within our culture Kujichagulia (Self Determination). Therefore, to all those students (some of who are now adults) and to their parents that I spoke to over the years, I sincerely appreciate your patience and perseverance. Here is your name book, *Original African American Names: Undefined.*

Dr. Adrienne N. Bryant

.

Original African American Names:

Undefined

Introduction

Original African American names represent a new genre in the naming lexicon. To be original by definition is to be creative. Original African American names epitomize creativity. Creativity in the human spirit is always inventing, reinventing and renewing part or all of what we have always known. Original African American names emerge from a human audacity to create something new, lasting and uniquely beautiful. Molefi Kete Assante, author of The *Book of African Names* explains, "Your name links you with your past, your ancestors and is a part of your spirituality. A beautiful name accompanies us for the rest of our life." Original African American names, as a name genre, pair the past denied native African languages with American English phonemic innovation. The result of this marriage is creative and beautiful names.

These non-traditional names or original African American names are acknowledged in two naming books on names for African American babies. In the book, *Proud Heritage: 11,001 Names for your African American Baby,* Elza Dinwddie-Boyd refers to these unique names as 'newly created' names. *Proud Heritage* devotes chapters to newly created names for boys and newly created names for girls. Another author, Teresa Norman, in her book, *The African American Baby Name Book*, identifies original African American names as 'American contemporary' names. In Norman's name book, original African American names are sorted with the other names in the text and the origin is identified as American contemporary. The names in both these name books are printed without meanings. The choice to include original names but have no meaning assigned allows for more meaningful and authentic definitions to be created.

In fact, for individuals, parents or naming surrogates with a connection to an original African American name there are no obstacles to choosing a meaning for their name. Original African American names are accepted in every aspect of American culture even without a particular definition. In the book, *100,000 Plus Baby Names* by Bruce Lansky includes hundreds original African American names. In this inclusive book the origin is identified as 'American'. These wonderful names are listed without a meaning. In the name book genre, original African American names are the most inimitable but would certainly be even more interesting with a definition or positive meaning.

Creators of original African American names developed these names without any preconceived context. Clearly the aim was to name a beloved new baby. However, newly created names and American contemporary names, intended or not, actually are tied to an historical construct. These names, in the context of the American experience, reveal an obvious link to creativity and hegemony. Hegemony is the dominating influence a group has over society or other groups of people. Our African American ancestors under American hegemony used imagination and inventiveness to improve their lives in the United States. It could be said that at long last, after decades of subjugation, a group of African Americans decided to reject the names of the dominate influence and create their own.

Original African American names are linked to ending a pattern of naming oppression. Naming oppression began on slave ships, was practiced on 19th century Native Americans and continued with 20th century immigrants. In the case of African Americans, a language lost people, to be able in some small way to regain naming; an act relegated to family (after the end of slavery) was indeed an accomplishment. American contemporary names, newly created names or original African American names represent a new naming genre and more. They represent a new beginning in American history for African Americans. Parents or naming surrogates consciously or innocently have created a new naming genre and a new connection to an African past.

This new beginning is characterized by self-empowerment. In essence, original African American names are reclaiming the ancestral practice of selecting names from one's own culture and defining one's self. Even in the absence of a mother tongue or language, African Americans have maniupulated English phonemes to create names to define themselves.

The making of this book, *Original African American Names: Undefined* echoes other events that enhance a constructive cultural connection. One such event is Kwanzaa. Maulana Karenga explains that "Kwanzaa is a synthesis of both continental Africans and Diasporan African cultural elements." *Original African American Names: Undefined* recognizes the influence of origins and experiences on African Americans in the Diaspora. Thus, selecting an original African American name is more than a new trend. Original African American names are an act of self determination and creativity that is grounded in an historical past.

Whereas, the African American past has been seemly broken with Mother Africa, original African American names repair the connection with an inventive new link. These new names represent a new beginning and deserve a positive meaning. Thus, the goal of this book, *Original African American Names: Undefined*, is to empower individuals with created names to add a positive meaning to their name. Once a good meaning is identified, individuals can celebrate and publish the meaning.

The naming ritual was a basic ritual practiced in many countries in Africa. As Africans, we celebrated the bestowing of a name with a positive meaning. Adopting a naming ritual that includes revealing the meaning of the name during a celebration, connects African Americans to a lost practice.

Everyone can benefit from thinking about themselves in terms of the most positive images. The bearers of original African American names and all in the human family can reflect on these questions. What does your name mean to you? What attributes do you want your name to carry into the future? The opportunity is given to you if you are the bearer of an original African

American name to discover your own meaning. If your name is *undefined* and undocumented, take these steps; 1. Define your name; 2. Share your story; and 3. Celebrate your name and its meaning.

The created meaning chosen from positive words or phrases necessitates documenting or recording. These meanings represent the greatest hope, aspiration, and love for the namee. The defining process is important but should not stop there. Each name naturally has a naming story. Naming stories are essential to understanding the historical paradigm shift from adopting names of others to embracing your own originality (or the originality of the individual bestowing an original African American name). In the absence of a griot to tell your story, the culminating act of self determination is to document the meaning and narrative associated with your original African American name.

This book, *Original African American names: Undefined*, is for everyone who has ever encountered a person with an unfamiliar name. Naming is our initiation into family, community, and society. As our human family enlarges we need to be prepared to engage and respect all names. Use this book to familiarize yourself with original names. Use this book as a talking point to encourage those with undefined original African American names to choose a meaning. If your name is recorded in this book, add your meaning and story for the next book. The next book will fulfill a promise to write a book with names, meanings and stories of original African American names.

This book, *Original African American Names: Undefined*, a partially fulfilled promise is both a resource and a reward. The book is a resource for those who know someone with an original name. The book, *Original African American names: Undefined* is a reward for those who now have positive recognition of their original African American name.

Here are a couple of reminders as you read through the following pages with lists of original African American names:

1. If you **do not** see your name, added it with an email to Dr. Bryant oaan2014@gmail.com.

2. If you see your name choose a meaning. Be prepared to supply verification that you are defining your name.

3. If you see a name in this book that has a known meaning, send an email to oaan2014@gmail.com. Be prepared to supply the title of the book documenting the name.

Finally, if you are so inclined, add your photo and voice video to the website www.originalafricanamericannames.com

From our ancestors come
our names, but from our
virtues comes our
honors. ~Proverb

List of Names

A *female*

Aayaisha
Afabiana
A'kahyla
A'laejah
A`layjah
Alekka
Alasia
Alleya
Allyessia
Almetha
Ameesha
Anaya
Anecia
Anntrysha
Anshenea
Antonella
Aolione
Ardishea
Aresia
Arjana
Arletta
Arrishae
Arshawana
Ashanae
A'Shane
Ayiana
AzJanea

ഇരു

To name
something is to
wait for it in the
place you think it
will pass.
Amiri Baraka
ഇരു

List of Names

A male

Ahjamond
Ajohn
Alvester
Amone
Anguez
Antwaunett
Antwoin
A`Shane
Avondre
Azhaunte

B female

Benion
Brashay
BreAnne
BreChelle
Brejonna

ꮟꮕꮳ
Before seeing her
son she named
him.
African Proverb
ꮟꮳ

B male

Brizjhane

C female

Calandra
Cea'Asia
Chamiya
Chaela
Chaniqua
Chaniya
Chanasia
Chardea

List of Names

C *female*

Charista
Charmaine
Charreah
Chatona
Chaynal
Chenelle
Chriscelle
Crischelle
Cristiona
Chyaharie
Chystia
Cuesta

C *male*

Chantz
Cherron
Chrishaun
Chrishawn
Cornez

D *female*

Da Chaleyce
Daemaurin
Daeosionae
DaeShavon
Daijanae
Dalynne
Da'mesha
Danajha

෨෧
A good name
shines in the dark.
African Proverb
෨෧

List of Names

D *female*

Danella
Darnay
Dasha
DaShawna
Dauryce
Davanta
DaZhane
DeAdria
DeAjahnique
Debretta
Dejana
Dejaunne
Dekistris
Delaja
Delessia
Demeshia
Denae
Deshalia
Desia
DeWanna
Deyondrah
DeZhane
Diamonique
Diauj
Diozanae
D`naya
D'Neah
Dynette

ജ൦ര
If you inherit a
name you must
also adopt its
affairs.
African Proverb
൦ඌ

List of Names

D male

Dabrion
DaeJon
Daemon
Daivohn
Da`Jon
Dakaurey
Damiane
D'Andre
Da'Neil
Da'Nell
DanShay
D'ante
D'Anzel
DaQuan,
Daray
Dariques
Darreontae
Da'Shaun
DaTrell
Dauryce
Davarious
DaVarus
Davion
DaVon
DaVonte
Davonte
Davounte`
Dawrence
De`Andre

ഊന്ദ
In order to find
evil-doers, every
human being is
given a name.
African Proverb
ഊന്ദ

List of Names

D male

Deaunte
Deauntea
Dedrique
DeEdward
Deion'dre
DeJon
De'Juan
Dekoven
Delawrence
Delonte
Delvin
Demarcus
Demaree
Demario
DeMarquese
Demaryius
DeMaurice
Demel
Demetrice
Deontate
Deontre
DeRae
Derion
Derron
Deshaun
Deshean
Deshon
DeShon
DeVaughn

ԑᗄᏻ
Names are given
to invite people.
African Proverb
ԑᗄᏻ

List of Names

D *male*

 DeVelle
 Dev'yon
 DeZhane
 Dezhant
 DiAnthony
 Dielleon
 Diondre
 Donate
 Dontray
 D'Ovion
 D'Vontre
 Dyrell

E *female*

 Elexxus
 Exzandra

F *female*

 Falesha
 Fauntanique
 Fayesha
 Fenetra

G *male*

 Generion
 Gjavion

I *female*

 I'Zavian

ഇ൙ര
He who has
named his child
'Stop Fighting'
does not make
bullets.
African Proverb
ഇ൙ര

List of Names

J   *female*

JaDawnya
Jadeus
Jaezell
Jahniyah
Ja'Honey
JaiLa
Ja'Kayla
Jakiyah
Jaleysa
Jalisa
Jalya
Jamesha
Jameye
Janae
Janay
Janaya
Janique
JaQuan
JaQuay
Jaquayla
Ja Quea
Jaquilla
Javalynn
Jaynaia
Je`nae
Jendaya
Jenell
Je'onn

৪০৫৪

A person takes his
name with him
wherever he goes.
African Proverb
৪০৫৪

List of Names

J *female*

Jerrae
Jerriem
Jesmyn
Jinnelle
Johnique
Jonasia
Jonea
Joneice
Jonesha
Jordainae
Jourday
Jo Vonka

J male

Jahron
Jai Quan
Jaisoun
Jakeese
Jakiyah
Jamal
Jamar
JaMarius
Jameelan
Jamel
Jamichael
Jammel
Ja'quaon
Jaquon
Jaryll

ଚ୍ଚେ
Every river than
runs into the sea
loses its name.
African Proverb
ଚ୍ଚେ

"Names, once they are in common use, quickly become mere sounds, their etymology being buried, like so many of the earth's marvels, beneath the dust of habit."
Salman Rushdie

List of Names

J *male*

Jatarrious
Javad
Javaughn
Javorris
Jawanza
Jawaun
Jawuan
Jayquawn
Jayon
JeQuale
Jermarcus
Jermichael
Jerrae
Jerrann
Jerraud
Jerrell
Jerren
Jerrickus
Jeshun
Jevonte
Jhaloni
Jibril
Jimelle
Joaquenssi
Jorane
Jorrele
Jovaris
Juaquin
Jyrese

List of Names

K female

Kalayshia
Kaleah
Kameelah
Karshella
Kauchinic
Kayandria
Kayz'onia
Keiyasha
Kendazzana
Kendrella
Kennise
Keona
Ke'sha
Keviyonna
Kh'miah
Kiacia
Kisha
Kniamiayah
Kurnesha
Kurtajsha
Kyree

ഔ൪ര
The name given to
a child becomes
natural to it.
African Proverb
ജ൪ര

K male

Kaderius
KaJandre
Kamerel
Kanique
Kayron
Kayvon

List of Names

K   male

Keauntea
KeDar
Kehiem
Keisean
Keishaun
Kentavious
Kenyan
Keschon
Keshay
Keshawn
Keshod
Keshon
Khayyam
Kisan
Knowshon
Kurvin
Kylear

ഇൻൽ
Your name was
known before you
came.
African Proverb
ഇൻൽ

L   female

LaChell
LaDonna
La Deja
LaDejah
Lajae
La'Jaye
Lakesha
Lakeya
Lakia
Lakitha

> "Names are not always what they seem. The common Welsh name BZJXXLLWCP is pronounced Jackson."
>
> Mark Twain

List of Names

L *female*

Lakyra
Lamoiselle
Lanesha
LaNise
Laparis
LaQuasha
LaQuueesha
Laquita
Larae
LaRai
Lariah
La Rischa
LaRita
LaSha
Lashai
LaShay
Lashay
LaShea
LaShundreya
Latasha
Latensia
LaTisha
Latisha
LaTonya
Latresea
LaTrice
Lavonne
LaWanda
LaZelle

List of Names

L *female*

Ledisi
Lenishia
LeOrna
Leshemia
LeVetta
Lilasha
Llauryn
Lonice
Lucritha
Luvern
Lynarica
Lytrice

L male

LaDarrius
Landen
Ladrea
Lavaris
Littrele

M female

MacKyla
Mahajzanay
Ma' jestic
Makayla
Malicea
Maquaja
Marcelite
Marjoya
Markesa

List of Names

M female

Marlesha
Marlicia
Marshae
MarShay
Michaelah
Myeasha
Myeisha
Myikaila
Myisha
Myquasia

M male

Markqual
Markuan
Marquan
Marshawne
Monie
Montaurius

N female

Nacreasha
NaDra
Nafeesha
Najalai
Nashea
Na'te
Nathzatauna
Nea'Asia

List of Names

N *female*

Nekeita
Nesselle
Nichelle
Nikiya
Niqualia
Ni'Que
Niqueeda
Niqualia
Nykeeisha
Nykeshia

N *male*

Nai'jae
NaQuan
Novaj

O *female*

Ondrelee
Oracene
Orathai
Oureana

O *male*

O'Derius

P *female*

Patshay
Phanesha
Phinaesha
Piea

ဆာ၆ဒ
He who is famous
has his name often
mentioned.
African Proverb
ဆ၆ဒ

List of Names

P *male*

Prathon

Q *female*

Quanta
Quayanna
Quiana
Quotesha
Quvenzhane

Q *male*

Q'Shaan
Quayshawn
Quevon
Quinndale
Quonta

⁖✓⁗
A good name is
better than riches.
African Proverb
⁖✓⁗

R *female*

Raavyn
Radora
Raelicia
Rae'Niek
Rajanique
Ralonda
Ramika
Ranisha
Rashacia
Raychell
Raynique
Rea'Asia
Reazjhana

List of Names

R female

Rebonnea
Re'Janae
ReMahnee
Renarda
Reneisha
Reshae
Rhyonha
Rickeesha
Rikkiana
R'Manie
Rochandra
Rodgeriqus
Roecia
Rushay

R male

Ramarley
Rayful
Rayshaan
Rayshawn
Resean
Rockeem
Rolaundo
Ronderrick
Ryshawn

"Society everywhere is
in conspiracy against
the manhood of every
one of its members.
The virtue in most
request is conformity.
Self-reliance is its
aversion. It loves not
realities and creators,
but names and
customs."
Ralph Waldo Emerson

List of Names

S *female*

Sammiah
Sareya
Shafae
Shafaye
Shahlia
Shakeyla
Shakira
Shakiyla
Shalayah
Shaleica
Shalyn
Shalynn
Shamaya
Shameka
Shanada
Shanae
Shanaz
Shandice
Shandella
Shaneen
Shanette
Shanice
Shanora
Shantae
Shantell
Shantoy
Shaqueda
Shaquille
Shaqwella

"It was Mom who, after naming Kamau, helped me understand the powerful energy of names. His name will be unique."
Maisha I

List of Names

S *female*

Sharamae
Sharhonda
Shariah
Sharika
Sharjuan
Sharlita
Shauique
Shaulonda
Shauntavia
Shauzme'ne
Shawnisha
Shawntez
Shayna
Shenika
Shaquea
Sherica
Sherika
Shrieka
Shykeitha
Stevisha
Synique

S *male*

Scheraun
Sen`Derrick
Semaj
Senoj
Shajuan
Shawntez

List of Names

T *female*

Tahrea
Tajianne
Ta'Jiona
Tajmia
TajShawnne
Takisha
Talisha
Tamae
Tamatri
Tamela
Tamika
Taneeka
Tanika
Taraya
TaRena
TaRhonda
Tasharina
Tatiyanna
Tazja
Teasia
Tiesha,
Trevesha
Tyauna
Tyiesha
Tyonka
Tyonna
Tyrongela
Tyshea
Tyshell

List of Names

T   male

Tahjlon

Tahrea

Taijon

Tarelle

Tashaun

Tranell

Travaris

Travon

Trayvon

Tra'Von

Tremayne

Tre Sean

Trevoughn

Trevante'

V   female

Vernika

Vontriece

W   female

Wilniqua

Wyndolyn

Y   female

Yashea

Z   female

Zaron

The Process

The process has taken me years to get going but it is simple. If you have an Original African American Name (OAAN) and you are 18 years or older please select a positive meaning for your name. There are some positive words in the back of this book. Then, submit that meaning for publication in the next book. If you are a parent or naming surrogate over age 18, you can submit a meaning for the child you named who is under age 18.

Many of you have interesting naming stories you would like to share and document in a book. Therefore, step two is to write down your empowering naming story and document that story for all to read. This is where you acknowledge people who were proud of you and protected you from the harm of hegemony in the American caste system.

An excellent meaning and powerful story needs a celebration. So finally announce and give yourself a party. Send out emails, use social media or hand write invitations to let the world know this is you. Whether it is a large celebration or an intimate celebration with friends and family just make it about your name, your meaning, and your story.

Bibliography

Asante,Molefi Kete. *The Book of African Names*. Trenton: Africa World Press, 1991.

Cheatham Bell, J. *Famous Black Quotations: and Some Not so Famous*. Chicago: Sabayt Publications, 1986.

Dinwiddie-Boyd, E. *Proud Heritage: 11,001 Names for Your African American Baby*. New York: Avon Books, 1994.

Karenga, Maulana. *Kwanzaa: A Celebration of Family, Community and Culture*. Los Angeles: University of Sankore Press, 2002.

Lansky, Bruce. *100,000 Plus Baby Names*. New York: Meadowbrook Press, 2009.

I, Maisha. *Journey to I Defiant, Defamed, Disgraced. . . My Unexpected Path to Success.* Denver, CO: Golden Dragon Press, 2014.

Norman, Teresa. *The African American Baby Name Book*. New York: Berkley Publishing, 1998.

Positive Words

abundance	comfortable	graceful
action	confident	gracious
admirable	consoler	harmony
adorable	cooperative	honest
adventurer	courageous	honorable
agreeable	curious	imaginative
alert	dashing	inquisitive
alive	dawn	intelligent
alluring	dazzling	invaluable
ambitious	debonair	inspiring
amused	decisive	jovial
aware	dedicated	joy
beautiful	delightful	jubilant
believer	devotion	keen
beloved	detailed	kind
benevolent	determined	knowing
blessed	diligent	laughter
brave	discreet	legacy
bright	dynamic	legendary
builder	elegant	lively
calm	eloquent	logical
capable	enterprising	loving
celebration	enthusiastic	loyal
charming	excel	magnificent
charismatic	flower	manly
cheerful	focused	merciful
clever	forgiveness	mercy
confident	friend	motivating
conscientious	generous	navigator
courageous	gentle	noble
cheerful	gift	open
coherent	goodness	opportunity

optimistic
one-hundred
percent
paradise
passionate
patient
perfect
perfection
persevere
philosopher
pleasing
popular
powerful
precious
pretty
principled
productive
progress
prominent
protected
proud
pure
quality
quiet
quick
rational
ready
reassuring
refined
refreshing
rejoice
reliable
remarkable

resounding
respected
respectful
responsible
restored
robust
ruler
safe
seemly
selective
self-assured
sensitive
sensuous
serene
shrewd
silly
sincere
skillful
smiling
splendid
steadfast
stern
stoic
strong
successful
talented
traveler
thoughtful
thrifty
tough
trustworthy
tranquil
transformative

trusting
truthful
unbiased
understanding
unwavering
unusual
upbeat
upright
upstanding
valor
valuable
valued
versatile
vibrant
vigorous
virtuous
vital
vivacious
warm
warrior
wealthy
whiz
willing
winner
wise
witty
wonderful
worthy
youthfulness
zeal
zealous
zestful
zenith

The Party List

The Party List

The party list was a list of invitees to my child's birthday party. The list of names came from my son's kindergarten teacher. I carried that list with me for over thirty years. Here are the names from that list that sparked my interest in unusual names 30 years ago (surnames omitted).

Corey
Shalona
Anthony
Torrence
Jamila
Erica
Bridget
Bryan
Mario
Martin
Christi
Mekisha
Safiyyah
Garreh
Okechukwu
Toure
Takiyah
Joseph
Steven
Nykita
Cory
Johnathan
Patrick
Natasha
Wilbur
Samuel
Adeginka

Original African American Names: Undefined

About the Author

Adrienne N. Bryant's career began in business. While working and attending school, she received a Bachelor of Business Administration from Central Oklahoma State University. She later earned a Master degree with teaching endorsement from Regis University in Denver. As a teacher leader, she wrote grants for her school and classroom, designed before and after school curriculum and programming, and led a successful African infused Summer School program. She ultimately earned a Ph.D. in Educational Leadership and Policy Studies from the University of Denver.

In her dissertation, *The Relationship between Teacher Qualification and Achievement of African American Middle School Students*, Dr Bryant writes:

> Teachers are a guiding force in translating the school
> curriculum that emerges from established educational policy.
> Policymakers, parents and teachers must empower all students
> with strategies to succeed, but educators must first be
> empowered with an understanding of the dynamics of
> stratification, dichotomy, inequity, and hegemony in America.
> There is an opportunity to relieve the anguish of failure by
> allowing authentic conversations that include positive ways to
> dismantle mandated oppressive educational practices and
> policies.

Dr. Bryant is an educator in a major urban school district. She was born in Seattle, Washington and has lived and traveled all over the United States and Africa. Dr. Bryant has five children, two grandchildren and enjoys quilting and gardening when she is not writing. Dr Bryant continues to challenge, channel and change young lives toward positive endeavors.

www.ingramcontent.com/pod-product-compliance
Lightning Source LLC
Chambersburg PA
CBHW070820290526
45795CB00002B/788